CCSS Genre Historical Fi

MW00464392

Essential Question
How do different groups contribute to a cause?

Norberto's HAT

BY SANDY MCKAY
ILLUSTRATED BY JAMES WATSON

CHAPTER 1

David Finds a Hat

CALIFORNIA, 1962

David Johnson stretched to reach his tennis racket in the hall closet. As he did so, a large, wide-brimmed hat tumbled out and fell on the floor beside him.

David's dad pounced on the hat. "I haven't seen this hat in years," he said, sounding surprised. "I thought it had been thrown out."

Dad ran his thumb along the soft, white felt, dirty with age and use. "This is a *sombrero*, and it belonged to your uncle Ralf," he said. "It must be around 20 years old by now."

"That's pretty old for a hat," said David.

"He was given it in 1943," said Dad, "during the Second World War."

"How old were you then?" David asked, realizing he had not spoken to his dad about the war much.

"Oh, not much older than you are now," said Dad, "about 14, if I remember correctly." He laughed, "Old enough to think I needed to leave school."

"*Fourteen*?" David couldn't imagine leaving school at 14. Right now, he felt as if he would probably be at school forever.

"Life was very different during the war," Dad continued. "So many young men were joining the forces. Laborers were difficult to find."

"The forces?" asked David.

"Army, navy, air force," Dad said, sitting down on the hall stairs. "I was too young to join, but not too young to work. A friend of mine had an uncle who owned a large sugar beet farm in central California a few hours from where we lived. He desperately needed workers and said we could come work for him."

Dad looked thoughtful. He added, "My father passed away when I was your age, so my mom had a lot to handle financially, and I guess I wanted to help out. I was officially the man of the house. I knew if I left school, I could earn some money."

"What did Gran think?" David asked.

"She wasn't happy about my leaving school, but she could see the sense in it. It was my contribution—people did what they could in those days."

David put down his tennis racket and took the sombrero. "So what does all that have to do with this hat?" he asked.

Dad ruffled David's hair. "Well, this sombrero originally belonged to a Mexican by the name of Norberto."

David liked the way his father pronounced the words *sombrero* and *Norberto*. He said them properly, as a Mexican would. David knew his dad could speak reasonably good Spanish, but he had never known why. Maybe now he would find out.

"Norberto came over the border from Mexico not long after the war started," Dad told David. "He came with many others to help American farmers with the harvest. Those Mexican men really stepped into the breach."

Dad took the hat from David and placed it on his own head as if it might help him to remember.

Then he settled back, closed his eyes, and took himself all the way back to 1943.

CHAPTER 2

Henry Meets Norberto

CALIFORNIA, 1943

Henry Johnson's mother stood at the kitchen sink washing the breakfast dishes. She was trying to get used to the idea that her eldest child was going away to work on a large sugar beet farm. She knew they needed the money, but it did not feel right for him to leave school at 14.

World War II had changed everything. People all around the world were saying farewell to their sons, uncles, fathers, and grandsons. Many from their own neighborhood had gone away, and Mrs. Johnson supposed she would just have to get used to it. At least she could be grateful that Henry was only 14. If he were four years older, he would be able to enlist. Compared with fighting in the army, work might not be such a bad option.

Two weeks later when Henry boarded a bus for the sugar beet farm, Mrs. Johnson waved good-bye reluctantly. After Henry left, she held tight to her younger children, Katy and Ralf.

As for Henry, he could not wait for his adventure to begin.

A few hours later the bus pulled up at the farm. Henry was hot, tired, and thirsty. The sugar beet fields stretched to the horizon in every direction. His eyes widened when he was taken to a small wooden shack. Inside was the bunk bed he would sleep on for the next six months.

The next day was even more of a shock. The work was harder than he had imagined. He began to realize that working up to ten hours a day in the hot sun would take some getting used to.

Henry shared the bunkhouse with his friends George and Chester. The Mexican workers, called *braceros*, camped in tents farther along. Stories abounded about how young Mexican men had lined up for days to get work across the border, grateful for the chance to earn money for their families back home.

Right from the start, Henry could see how physically fit and skillful the Mexicans were. He had never met anyone from Mexico before. He was fascinated by the way these men looked—the diversity of their clothes and the sound of their language.

The braceros often gathered together after the sun went down to play their music and sing. Some of them were accomplished guitar players, and Henry, George, and Chester loved to lie in their bunks listening to the haunting melodies.

After work, the young boys would sometimes walk down past the braceros' camp to the swimming hole on the east side of the farm.

Henry sympathized with the braceros. He could only imagine how difficult their life must be such a long way from home. He was wary of them as well, however, probably because they were different. Not understanding the language they spoke sometimes made him feel afraid.

One night, when Henry and George were out walking, they started talking about the war. George's dad was a pilot in the air force and had to perform dangerous military operations. George was proud of him, but he worried about his dad's safety. The boys did not receive many letters out here, and it was hard to keep up with news bulletins on the farm.

Henry became so engrossed in the conversation that he did not notice his wallet slip out of the pocket of his trousers. It was only after he got back to the bunkhouse that he discovered his wallet was gone.

At first, Henry thought he must have dropped his wallet outside the bunkhouse, but when he retraced his steps, he found nothing. With a feeling of rising panic, he retraced his steps again—still no sign of the wallet. The farm manager was not any help. When Henry asked him if anyone had found it, he replied with a yawn, "One of the braceros has probably pocketed it."

"But how will I get it back?" Henry asked anxiously.

The manager shrugged. "Don't count on getting it back."

Henry felt sick with worry. The wallet contained two weeks' wages, and he knew his mom would be devastated. Henry fretted about it all night until his stomach was in knots. He did not like the way the manager had assumed a bracero had kept his wallet, but could the manager have a point?

The next evening, George and Henry were walking past the braceros' camp when they heard someone whistle. They turned around to see a Mexican boy not much older than them. He wore a white, wide-brimmed hat and the biggest smile you ever saw. In his hand was a brown leather wallet.

The bracero grinned and handed the wallet to Henry, who immediately checked for his money inside. When he saw it was still there, he felt himself blush.

He shook the bracero's hand. "Thank you, but ... how did you know it was mine?"

"*La foto,*" the bracero said. He pointed to the photograph and then to Henry. "*Es una foto de su familia.*"

"He recognized you from your family photograph," explained George, who knew a little Spanish.

The bracero said something else in Spanish.

"Now he wants to show you *his* family photo," said George.

The bracero reached into his back pocket and brought out a small, tattered photograph of his family. He began to recite the names one by one: "*Mamá, Papá, Fidel* ..." Then he pointed at Henry's photograph, encouraging him to name his family, too.

The boys sat under the tree sharing photographs. In half an hour, Henry knew how to say Mom and Dad in Spanish. He also knew how to say Norberto, the bracero's name, the proper Mexican way.

Then Henry had a thought. "Can you teach me Spanish?" he asked.

Norberto grinned, "*Sí.*"

CHAPTER 3

A Guest for Dinner

CALIFORNIA, 1943

Henry and Norberto met every night. As the days wore on, not only did Henry's Spanish improve—almost as much as Norberto's English—but he also got used to the exhausting work. It was a matter of survival, and at least he knew he could return home every second weekend. The braceros were only allowed to leave the farm once a month.

One day, Henry had an idea. To repay Norberto's kindness, he would invite Norberto home with him.

Mrs. Johnson, Katy, and Ralf were waiting for the two boys to arrive. Henry had odd new feelings coming home. Sometimes he felt as if he had never been away, and sometimes he felt like a stranger.

Once inside, Norberto took off his hat and placed it on the chair. His copper skin and sleek black hair put him in stark contrast to the Johnsons, who were fair skinned and blond.

After half an hour, Norberto was chatting away like one of the family.

"Can I try on your hat?" Ralf asked.

"*Sí, sí,*" said Norberto.

After dinner, everyone went out to the front porch to talk. Norberto spoke about his brother, Fidel. "I think he is the same age as you, Ralf," he said.

"I'm 12 and a half," said Ralf proudly.

"Ah!" said Norberto. "I thought so."

Norberto told them how much he missed his family. They were astounded to learn that he had not been home to Mexico in more than a year!

The next morning, as Norberto and Henry got ready to leave, Mrs. Johnson said, "We're all so grateful for the work you are doing, Norberto. Who knows how the crops would get harvested if it weren't for the braceros."

Norberto smiled and said *Gracias*," but then he frowned. He said that he'd be a lot happier if he were certain of his money getting back home each month. He explained that the courier was not very reliable and sometimes the money did not get to his family.

Mrs. Johnson told Norberto he should send it by certified mail to prevent it from being intercepted. She explained to him that he just needed to fill out a form at the post office.

Norberto nodded and said he understood.

"Please come again, Norberto," said Mrs. Johnson as she waved good-bye.

CHAPTER 4

Hat Swap

CALIFORNIA, 1943

Norberto and Henry returned to the sugar beet farm, and the warm weather continued. Henry had never worked so hard in his life—gathering, sorting, and packing the beets. The braceros worked even harder, thinning out row after row of sugar beets with short-handled hoes.

A month later, Henry brought Norberto home with him again. Mrs. Johnson wanted to know if his family had received their money.

"Money? Oh, yes. *Sí.*" Norberto's face lit up. "*Sí, gracias.*"

Like last time, they sat around talking after dinner. Again, Ralf could not take his eyes off Norberto's hat.

This time, as they were leaving, Norberto smiled and handed his hat to Ralf. "My sombrero, you take my sombrero!"

Surprised, Ralf said, "Oh, no! I couldn't take your hat, Norberto. How will you work without your hat?"

Norberto shrugged. "I can get another hat," he said.

Suddenly Ralf grinned. "You can have mine, and I'll have yours," he said, racing off to get his favorite dark green cap. Norberto smiled, delighted. They all agreed that Ralf's cap suited Norberto very well.

CALIFORNIA, 1962

David put on Norberto's hat and imagined Uncle Ralf wearing it. "So what happened next? Did you and Norberto keep working together?" he asked his father.

Dad's eyes clouded. "Sadly, no," he said. "Soon after that, the sugar beet harvest was in. Norberto moved to a different farm, and I returned home. Ralf gave me the sombrero a few years after I got back. He said his head had grown too big and it wouldn't fit him." Dad laughed.

"I wrote to Norberto once, but the letter came back. The funny thing is, I did see Ralf's green cap again."

"Really? Where?" asked David.

"We came upon a group of Mexican braceros about a year later, near where I lived," Dad said. "They looked like new recruits, and one of them was wearing the same green cap—it stood out. I made my mother stop the car. The person wearing it obviously wasn't Norberto, but there was a resemblance. So I asked him where he got the cap."

"What did he say?" asked David.

"He said his brother gave it to him. The boy's name was Fidel. He was Norberto's younger brother. It was so good to meet him, and I asked him to give my regards to his big brother."

Dad smiled fondly at this memory and told David "I'll always be grateful to those braceros."

Respond to Reading

Summarize

Use the most important details from *Norberto's Hat* to summarize the story. Your graphic organizer may help you.

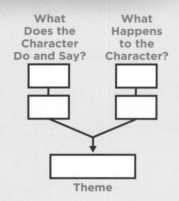

What Does the Character Do and Say?

What Happens to the Character?

Theme

Text Evidence

1. What features of the text help you identify it as historical fiction? **GENRE**

2. What is the "cause" in *Norberto's Hat*? How did different groups in the story contribute to that cause? **THEME**

3. On page 3, the word *beet* sounds the same as the word *beat*, but they have different meanings. What is the meaning of *beet*? Use context clues to help you. Then find another pair of homophones on page 10. **HOMOPHONES**

4. Write about the attitude of Mrs. Johnson and Henry Johnson toward the braceros. How do their statements help convey the author's message? **WRITE ABOUT READING**

Compare Texts

Read about Mexicans who worked on farms to help the United States during World War II.

THE Bracero Program

When the United States entered World War II, many young men joined the armed forces. This resulted in a significant labor shortage, especially in agriculture. The loss of workers was a major problem. A good food supply was important to the war effort. Without enough workers, how would farmers harvest their crops?

In 1942, the U.S. Secretary of Agriculture traveled to Mexico City. He spoke with the Mexican government about employing Mexican workers on U.S. farms.

The resulting Bracero Program seemed like a good solution for both countries. Mexico was suffering hard economic times, and the program gave strong, unmarried men from poor rural areas the opportunity to earn money for themselves and their families.

By 1945, there were more than 50,000 braceros employed in U.S. agriculture.

Mexican workers embraced the opportunity, and many lined up for days in an effort to be included in the program. Although not everyone was accepted, huge numbers of young Mexican men arrived in towns near the U.S. border, hoping to be chosen.

During the Bracero Program, more than 4.6 million contracts were signed with Mexicans who crossed the border to work.

Life for the braceros was not easy. They labored tirelessly on large farms and worked in difficult conditions picking cucumbers and tomatoes, thinning sugar beets, and weeding and picking cotton.

They worked long hours, often from daybreak to past sundown. Many workers suffered homesickness because they weren't allowed to return home until the end of their contracts.

There were rules to protect the braceros regarding pay rates, decent housing, affordable meals, and transportation back to Mexico. Not every employer followed these rules, however.

The Bracero Program lasted for 22 years (1942–1964). Today the legacy of the braceros remains important. These hardworking men helped to make American agricultural fields some of the most productive in the world.

A BRACERO REMEMBERS

Jesús Campoya Calderón, from San Diego, Chihuahua, Mexico, remembers his time as a bracero:

"In the farms we would do anything, although our permit was to pick cotton only."

The picker got $2.10 for 100 pounds of cotton. The best cotton picker made $31.40 in a good week.

"Sounds low, but then a pair of authentic Levi's jeans cost $1.98 …"

Once a week, the braceros were taken into town to buy groceries and supplies. Sometimes they used the opportunity to send money home.

"Because I didn't trust the bank, I saved all my money for myself. I worked four months, seven days a week, at least 12 hours every day, and I took home almost $300."

Make Connections

Why did the United States need Mexican farm workers during World War II? **ESSENTIAL QUESTION**

Using *Norberto's Hat* and *The Bracero Program* for evidence, explain why the braceros wanted to work on American farms and what life was like for the laborers. **TEXT TO TEXT**

Focus on Literary Elements

Flashbacks Flashbacks can be used in both fiction and nonfiction. They are parts of a text that tell what happened in an earlier time from the main story or article.

Flashbacks can provide background about a character or event. The writer often lets the reader know that the story is about to go back in time by having a character pause to retell or recall events from the past. A flashback can be long or short. It can be separated in a chapter or be part of the main text.

Read and Find In *Norberto's Hat*, Chapter 1 is set in 1962. At the end of the chapter, Dad "closed his eyes, and took himself all the way back to 1943." The next chapter is set in 1943 when Dad (Henry Johnson) was 14 years old.

The flashback continues until near the end of Chapter 4 when we return to 1962 and Dad tells David about an event in 1944.

Your Turn

Think about Norberto. How might he think about those war years when he worked on farms in California, far away from his family in Mexico?

Write a short flashback from Norberto's point of view, describing how Norberto met Henry and how he felt about his contribution to the U.S. war effort.